D1473993

O. Vandeputte / P. Vincent / T. Hermans

The language of twenty million Dutch and Flemish people

Published by the
Flemish-Netherlands Foundation «Stichting Ons Erfdeel vzw»
1986

People often directly associate the name of a country with that of a language. French is the language of France, English that of England, German that of Germany. It seems simple and practical. In reality, however, the assumption reflects a rather simplistic view of the relation between the languages and nations of Europe. In many cases the name of a country bears no relation to the name of the language or languages spoken in that country. There is no such thing as a Belgian language, or a Swiss, or Austrian, or Yugoslav language ...

The linguistic map of Europe gets distorted in another way, too. People who are aware that Belgium and Switzerland have no language of their own and that French is spoken in both countries, are apt to forget that in Belgium the Dutch-speakers and in Switzerland the German-speakers constitute the majority of the population (more than 60 %, in fact).

But what do terms like „majority" and „minority" mean in a European context? Strictly speaking, there is no majority language in Europe. No one language is spoken by more than fifteen per cent of all Europeans as their native tongue, so that Europe contains nothing but minority languages. And if we confine ourselves to single nations, we find that a language which is a minority language in one country may well be the language of the majority across the border. Obvious examples are French in Belgium and in Switzerland, or German in Belgium and in Italy: minority languages in one country, majority languages in another. In dealing with the languages of Europe, one fundamental point should never be overlooked: national frontiers and language frontiers by no means always coincide.

The question of where Dutch is spoken also raises problems concerning the name both of the language itself and of the area where it is used. Among linguists writing in English the recently-coined neologism „Netherlandic" is used synonymously with „Dutch" (the term „Netherlandish", despite its long and respectable pedigree, is only current in art-history). On the other hand it is not uncommon to hear the standard language of Flanders (in its broader meaning of Dutch-speaking Belgium, see below) referred to as „Flemish", which is then sometimes thought to be a mixture of Dutch and French. Others assume that Dutch is roughly the same as Low German. In addition, English usage tends to treat the geographical terms „Holland", „The Netherlands" and „the Low Countries" as somehow interchangeable. A few preliminary distinctions and definitions are necessary to clear up this terminological confusion.

The Netherlands

In its widest *geographical* application the term „Netherlands" denotes the lowlands of north-western Europe, encompassing the present-day kingdoms of the Netherlands and Belgium, the Grand-Duchy of Luxemburg, and northern France as far as the river Somme. In this geographical sense „Netherlands" is synonymous with „Low Countries". *Historically* speaking it is the collective name for the various regions in the Scheldt-Meuse-Rhine delta which, in the 14th and 15th centuries, were united into a single political entity under the dukes of Burgundy. It subsequently became the name of the kingdom which from 1815 until 1830 comprised, under William I, Belgium and the Grand-Duchy of Luxemburg as well as the present-day Netherlands.

At present the term refers to the Kingdom of the Netherlands, with Amsterdam as its capital. In Dutch we speak of „Nederland" or „Koninkrijk der Nederlanden" (Kingdom of the Netherlands).

Holland

In popular parlance - but never in official documents - the Kingdom of the Netherlands is often called Holland, a reference to the two provinces (North and South Holland) which after the revolt against Spain in the 16th century rose to economic and cultural prominence within the Dutch Republic. To speak of Holland while referring to the whole of the Netherlands is to use a figure of speech, a *pars pro toto,* the part for the whole. This figure of speech is by no means unique as regards the names given to particular countries. England is a case in point, as it takes its name from only one of the Germanic tribes (namely the Angles, in Old English: „Engle") who settled in the British Isles in the 5th and 6th centuries A.D.

Flanders

The use of the term „Flanders", too, is often confused and confusing. As a *geographical* region Flanders consists of the Belgian provinces of East and West Flanders, French-Flanders (in France), and Zealand-Flanders (in The Netherlands). *Historically* speaking Flanders is a county, most of which was a fief of the King of France; at the moment of its greatest expansion (in the 10th century

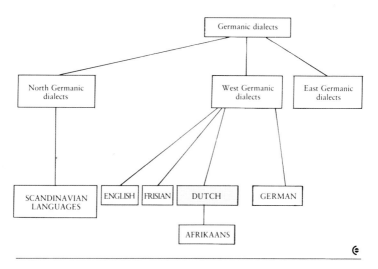

The Germanic dialects belong to the Indo-European family of languages, which also includes the Indo-Iranian, Albanian, Slavonic, Greek, Romance and Celtic dialect-groups. Long before the start of the Christian era the Germanic dialects acquired characteristic features, among them the placing of word stress on the first syllable.

By 400 A.D. a further differentiation had occurred within the Germanic dialect-group. Three main sub-groups emerged:

1) The East Germanic dialects, all of which have become extinct (Gothic, Vandalic and Burgundian).

2) The North Germanic dialects, from which the Scandinavian languages (Norwegian, Icelandic, Swedish and Danish) developed.

3) The West Germanic dialects, comprising on the one hand the Inguaeonic dialects (from which English and Frisian derive), and on the other the Continental Germanic dialects: firstly the Dutch dialects, secondly the Low German ones, and thirdly the High German dialects. Modern Standard German emerged from the High German dialects and has also become the standard language of the Low German dialect-area in Germany. In South Africa Afrikaans developed from the Dutch of seamen and farmers from the provinces of Holland and Zealand.

A.D.) it comprised East and West Flanders, Zealand-Flanders and the North of France as far as the Somme.

In the *present-day* political context the term „Flanders" (in Belgium) denotes that part of Belgium which lies to the north of the Dutch-French language border (see the map on the cover). The Language Laws of 1963 officially laid down this line of demarcation. The provinces of West and East Flanders, Antwerp and Limburg lie entirely to the north of the line and within the Dutch-speaking area, while the provinces of Hainault, Namur, Luxemburg and Liège lie entirely to the South of it and within the French-speaking area. The central province of Brabant is cut in two by the language border. Its northern half, Flemish Brabant, is Dutch-speaking, and the remainder, Walloon Brabant, is French-speaking.

Brussels, the capital of Belgium, is a special case. It is officially bilingual (Dutch and French), and constitutes a bilingual enclave in the exclusively Dutch-speaking area of Flemish Brabant. The dialect of Brussels is Dutch in origin and still alive, although it has been strongly influenced by French. In the course of the last century and a half, i.e. since Belgian independence, tens of thousands of Walloons have taken up residence in Brussels, as civil servants or high-ranking employees in firms. Considerable numbers of Flemings, too, have migrated to Brussels, but until recently they came almost exclusively from the poorer and less influential classes of the population. Under heavy social pressure and the added influence of the educational system and the administration, many of them adopted French as their medium of expression, a trend which seems to have come to a halt now.

Area of Continental German dialects

High German dialect area

Low German dialect area

Area with German as an official language

Area with Dutch as an official language

Modern Standard German derives from the dialects to the south of the line Aachen-Frankfurt a.d. Oder, i.e. from the dialects which participated in the High German sound shift.

Dutch has its origins in the West Germanic dialects of the Scheldt-Rhine-Meuse delta, dialects which were unaffected by the High German sound shift.

German and Dutch are therefore not only geographically but also linguistically differentiated.

The nucleus of the German language-area comprises the Federal Republic of Germany, the German Democratic Republic, Austria, and German-speaking Switzerland. In addition there are German-speaking minorities in many neighbouring countries, showing clearly that national frontiers and linguistic boundaries do not always coincide.

Terms like „The Netherlands", „Holland", and „Flanders", then, all have a range of meanings. Considering the history of the Scheldt-Meuse-Rhine delta, this is not surprising. Not until 1815 did the national boundaries in this part of the world become fixed (the eastern borders excepted, though the changes affecting these have not had any influence on the various designations applied to the delta region).

The entire area known today as The Netherlands and Flanders (in Belgium) has one standard language: Dutch. This language is for Flanders and The Netherlands what French is for France: the official language of the media and the administration, and of education and culture.

Dutch and German

The Dutch language, like German, English, Swedish, Norwegian, Danish and Icelandic, developed out of Germanic dialects. Of these dialects, the High German ones have the most clearly distinguished consonant system. By way of comparison:

Dutch: a*pp*el and aa*p*, *t*wee and e*t*en, boe*k*

English: a*pp*le and a*p*e, *t*wo and ea*t*, boo*k*

German: A*pf*el and A*ff*e, *z*wei (z = [ts]) and e*ss*en, Bu*ch* (ch = [x])

In the High German dialects the original Germanic consonants [p], [t], and [k], respectively developed into [pf] or [f], [ts] or [s], and [x]. In Dutch and English dialects this development did not take place. Another conspicuous difference is the change from original Germanic

[d] into [t] in at least a number of High German dialects. Compare, e.g., Dutch „dag" and English „day" with High German „Tag". The so-called High German sound shift began in the southern part of the West Germanic language-area, more particularly in northern Italy. It spread northwards across the Alps, affecting the dialects of Switzerland, Austria and southern Germany, and penetrating as far as central Germany. It came to a halt on the line Aachen-Düsseldorf-Kassel-Magdeburg-Frankfurt a.d. Oder. The process was complete by the end of the 8th century A.D. (see the map on p. 10).

Modern Standard German developed out of the High German dialects, i.e. the dialects to the south of the line Aachen-Frankfurt a.d. Oder, which had all undergone the sound shift. This is the language of Martin Luther's Bible translation. Before the end of the 16th century it had become the written language („Schriftsprache") used by the Church, the schools and universities, and the leading printers. In the course of the 18th and 19th centuries this High German standard language - we now simply call it German - also became the everyday speech of the upper classes in those areas to the north of the line Aachen-Frankfurt a.d. Oder which formed part of the German Empire, i.e. areas with Low German dialects unaffected by the sound shift.

Whereas modern German has its roots in southern and central Germany, Dutch developed out of the Germanic dialects spoken in the delta of the great rivers. The difference between Dutch and German, in other words, is a linguistic as well as a geographical one (see also Appendix 1).

The designation „Nederlands" („Netherlandic", i.e. Dutch) appears for the first time in 1482, in a rare incunable from Gouda. It never fell into disuse, but for a long time a number of other designations existed alongside it. The term „Nederlands" gained the upper hand only in the late 19th and early 20th century.

Before 1482 the Germanic dialects of the areas on both sides of the North Sea were known in Latin as „theodiscus", or, in the local dialects themselves, as „dietsch" or „duutsch" (later: „duytsch"), names which have survived in the terms „Deutsch" (German) and „Dutch". „Dietsch" means: of the „diet", or people. The term was used to distinguish the Germanic dialects from Latin and from the „Walloon" or foreign (i.e. French) dialects.

In the opening lines of the 13th-century animal epic *Van den Vos Reynaerde* (Reynard the Fox), one of the masterpieces of medieval Dutch literature, the author informs us that the story of Reynard's adventures was left unfinished in „Dietsch", and that he will therefore continue it, after „the French books":

> *Willem took it much to heart*
> *That one adventure of Reynard*
> *In Dutch remained as yet untold (…)*
> *For that legend he made a search*
> *And began to tell it in Dutch*
> *After the French in which it was made.*

(E. Colledge, ed.: *Reynard the Fox and Other Netherlands Secular Literature,* translated by A.J. Barnouw and E. Colledge. London, Heinemann, 1967)

13

Jacob van Maerlant
(1225-after 1291).

Reynard the Fox.

entity. This „Burgundian Circle" comprised roughly the present-day Benelux countries, but without Liège and with a substantial part of what is now Northern France, namely the county of Artois and the region around Cambrai (in Hainault). Charles V's Pragmatic Sanction of 1549 declared the „Circle" to be one indivisible whole, with the same succession rights applying jointly to all the provinces. The Seventeen Provinces, then, included the entire Dutch-speaking area (as well as some French-speaking parts, in the South). Although still linked to the Habsburg Empire, they had their own legal and judicial system. The awareness among the „Netherlanders" of being different from the rest of the Habsburg Empire found expression in the name they were to use henceforth for their language: apart from „Dietsch" and „Duutsch", „Nederduytsch" and „Nederlandsch" came into use. The term „Nederduytsch" (literally: „Nether-Dutch", i.e. the „duutsch" or „duytsch" of the Netherlands, as opposed to that of Germany) emphasized the difference between Dutch and (High) German. The term „Nederlandsch" („Netherlandic") left no room for confusion at all.

Joas Lambrecht's book *Néderlandsche Spellijnghe* (Dutch Spelling) appeared in 1550. A few years later Jan van den Werve published a word-list under the title *Het Tresoor der Duytsscher Talen* (A Thesaurus of the Dutch Language), and in 1584 the first grammar of Dutch, Hendrik Laurensz. Spiegel's highly influential *Twe-spraack vande Nederduitsche Letterkunst* (A Dialogue on the Dutch Language), saw the light. In this way the terms „Duytsch", „Nederduytsch" and „Nederlandsch" existed side by side from the 16th century onwards. Only in the early 20th century did „Nederlands" (the modern spelling of „Nederlandsch") finally outstrip its competitors.

The religious upheavals of the 16th century had momentous consequences for the Low Countries and their language. In 1566 the Calvinist-inspired „Iconoclastic Fury" broke out in Steenvoorde (in what is now French-Flanders, see Appendix 2). Churches were desecrated, their windows and statues smashed, garments and books burnt. Within the space of a few weeks the revolt fanned out across the Netherlands. When Philip II received the news in Spain, he dispatched the Duke of Alva to the Low Countries to avenge the ignominy which Spain and the Catholic Church had suffered. Alva's repression of the Protestants was of the utmost harshness. He installed a Council of Troubles, which pronounced countless death sentences (the popular Counts of Egmont and Hoorne were among the first to be executed, in the centre of Brussels, in 1568).

The political and military attempts by William the Silent to preserve the unity of the Low Countries proved ultimately unsuccessful. While elite troops under Alexander Farnese reconquered the Southern and Eastern regions, the Northern provinces held out. Antwerp fell to the Spaniards in 1585. When the Northern provinces subsequently blockaded the Scheldt, the great days of the port of Antwerp and of the Brabant area were over.

The separation of North and South had become a fact, but the struggle between the Spanish-dominated South and the rebellious United Provinces in the North was not finished yet. The counter-offensive of the United Provinces lasted until 1648, when the Treaty of Munster was concluded. Spain recognized the independence of the

Dutch Republic and the border between the northern and southern halves of the Low Countries (which more or less coincides with the present border between the Netherlands and Belgium). Trade with the Indies was forbidden to the South, and the Scheldt remained closed.

The emergence of Standard Dutch

By the end of the 16th century tens of thousands had already left the Southern Provinces for the North. For political, economic, or religious reasons, they refused to resign themselves to Spanish rule. Many settled in Zealand, more still in Holland, and particularly in Amsterdam. Holland's Golden Age is to a considerable extent the work of these immigrants. The Amsterdammer Joost van den Vondel (1587-1679), „Prince of Dutch Letters", was born in Cologne, but his parents came from Antwerp. Franciscus Gomarus, the spokesman of the hardline Calvinists who carried the day at the Synod of Dordrecht in 1618-19, was born in Bruges. Lieven de Key, from Ghent, became the master builder of Haarlem. Daniel Heinsius, also from Ghent, was one of the most respected philologists at the University of Leyden. Willem Usselincx, from Antwerp, masterminded the establishment of the West India Company. The mathematician and military engineer Simon Stevin, from Bruges, became tutor to William the Silent's son, Maurice of Nassau, and later managed the Prince's finances. These random examples may suffice to show that the division of the Low Countries meant a severe blood-letting for the South.

Not a few of these Southern immigrants were well-to-do people, and when they came they brought not only

The „States Bible", printed in 1637 at Leyden

experience and know-how, but also money and social prestige. It is not surprising that their language, too, enjoyed a similar standing, all the more so since the written language had always been distinctly Southern in character.

However, it was in Holland, where thousands of Flemings and Brabanters had taken refuge, that Standard Dutch found its definitive shape. The influence of Amsterdam on modern Standard Dutch has been paramount. „No other town in Holland has attracted so many immigrants both from the Netherlands and abroad since the end of the 16th century, no other town has had such a profound impact on the formation of Standard Dutch as it is spoken and written today." (Jo Daan, in *Onze Taal* (Our Language), XLIV, 4, 1975, p. 17).

Other towns, like The Hague and Haarlem, also became centres of literary activity, and 1637 saw the publication of the States Bible in Leyden. The translation had been commissioned by the supreme authority of the Republic, the States-General, and was based on the original Greek and Hebrew, rather than on the Latin Vulgate, which most previous translators had used. Detailed instructions had been issued, one of them stipulating that expressions and turns of phrase which occurred in the original languages were to be rendered literally wherever possible. This instruction left its mark on the translation, and thus influenced the vocabulary and figurative usage of written Dutch.

Among the translators were men from all parts of the Netherlands, including Southern immigrants. The close contacts between them resulted in a kind of hybrid language, of which the States Bible furnishes ample

Joost van den Vondel
(1587-1679).

PIETER CORNELISZ HOOFT,
Ridder van S.' Michiel, Droſt te Muyden, Baljuw van Goeilant . &c.

Pieter Corneliszoon Hooft
(1581-1647).

evidence. But a similar mixture of linguistic forms may be observed in other domains, too. Both the upper classes and men of letters began to rid their language of regional features. Following a long-established practice, Northern writers made their language conform to the Southern literary tradition. One such author was P.C. Hooft (1581-1647), whose work contributed in great measure to the development of classical Dutch. At the same time the Flemings and Brabanters - Joost van den Vondel among them - adjusted their language to suit the new linguistic environment. In this way the prototype of modern written Dutch came into being.

Spoken language

And the spoken language? The great majority of Hollanders simply continued to speak their local dialect, but the upper classes, native Hollanders and Southern immigrants alike, showed a growing tendency towards uniformity, resulting in a kind of mixed language predominantly based on the dialect of Holland but containing many Southern elements as well. This mixed language was subsequently adopted by educated people in the other provinces of the Republic.

The stylistic rift between the written language, with its unmistakeable Renaissance and Southern imprint, and the spoken language, shaped essentially by the dialect of Holland, has to an extent survived down to the present day. The 19th-century Dutch writer Eduard Douwes Dekker was the first to try and bridge this gap (under the pseudonym Multatuli he wrote the masterly novel *Max Havelaar*, 1860, a virulent denunciation of colonialism).

Multatuli (Eduard Douwes Dekker, 1820-1887).

He wanted the written language to sound more „natural", more in accord with the spoken idiom. His work heralded the rejuvenation of Dutch prose, and gave impetus to a gradual and still-continuing rapprochement between speech and writing both in literary and general usage.

The South after the separation; the 17th and 18th centuries

The Republic of the United Provinces did not comprise the entire Dutch-speaking area. After the period of Spanish domination (1598-1713), the Southern provinces were for a time under Austrian rule (1713-1792), and in 1794 came the French. As early as the 17th century sizeable parts of the Netherlands - Artois, and parts of Flanders - had been lost to France. Under the Spanish, the Austrians and the French, the language of the administration in the Southern Netherlands, even in those areas where dialects of Dutch were spoken, was not Dutch, but French. Thus, as a result of foreign domination, the social gap between the higher and lower strata of the population was expressed in terms of an opposition between languages, a social language-barrier. Whereas ordinary people used their (Dutch) dialect, the upper classes spoke French, became French-speaking, or pretended to be. To speak French meant power and prestige.

Whereas in the North the Dutch language steadily developed both in its written and in its spoken form, in the South there was only stagnation, and the language broke up into an amalgam of purely local forms. The Southern provinces did not produce any writers of note in the 17th and 18th centuries, and those from the Republic

Willem I, King of the Netherlands (1772-1843).

in the North were not sufficiently known south of the border to serve as models for a more general linguistic norm. The only Southern writer worth mentioning in this period is Michiel de Swaen (1654-1707), who lived in Dunkirk, a town which had become a French possession in 1662, but which culturally was to remain part of the Netherlands until long afterwards.

Dutch as the language of the United Kingdom of the Netherlands under William I (1815-1830)

Following upon Napoleon's defeat at Waterloo, and after more than 200 years of separation, the Southern Netherlands and the United Provinces were joined together to form the United Kingdom of the Netherlands under William I. The national language of the newly-created state was to be Dutch - the mother tongue of some 75 % of the total population. Such was the logic of those days: William I's rulings simply replaced the authoritarian decrees of the French, and Dutch was to be the language of the realm, although not in so thoroughgoing a fashion as French in the French Republic or the French Empire. This did not mean that Wallonia was also to be made Dutch-speaking, but that Dutch was to replace French as the preferred language of the central administration.

In 1819 the government issued a decree designed to make Dutch, from 1823 onwards, the only official language of the (Flemish) provinces of East and West Flanders, Antwerp and Limburg. Four years later the decree was extended to cover the Flemish part of the province of Brabant (the districts of Louvain and Brussels). For a short time it looked as if Dutch would become the official tongue in the entire area where dialects of Dutch were

Hendrik Conscience
(1812-1883).

Guido Gezelle
(1830-1899).

specialists. The Provisional Government leaves this task to the local authorities." By „Flemish dialects" he meant of course all the Dutch dialects in Belgium (i.e. those of Brabant and Limburg as well as of Flanders in the narrow sense).

The Age of Romanticism, however, expressed itself not only in the rebellion against William I. In Flanders it also stimulated a revaluation of the national past and a renewed interest in the language - a language seriously threatened by the government's pro-French policies. In 1838 Hendrik Conscience, the son of a Flemish mother and a French father, published the influential historical novel *De Leeuw van Vlaanderen* (The Lion of Flanders), an epic description of the heroism of the Flemish armies which defeated the French aristocracy at the Battle of the Golden Spurs in 1302.

At first the Flemish radicals were not agreed on exactly what idiom was eventually to be the official language of Flanders side by side with or in place of French. There was no general „Flemish" language over and above the various local dialects of Northern Belgium. The term „Flemish" (Dutch: „Vlaams"; French: „flamand") had some currency, but it simply stood for the sum total of Dutch dialects which still flourished in the northern half of Belgium and which were regarded by some as a sufficient base, or at least a substitute, for a Flemish standard language, provided they were drained of exclusively local words, turns of phrase and pronunciation.

The so-called „localists" advocated such a specifically Flemish standard language. One of their spokesmen was the West Flemish poet Guido Gezelle (1830-1899), who campaigned in favour of a language rooted in the

Jan Frans Willems (1793-1846).

ancient strata underlying the diversity of Dutch dialects. In this respect the conservative West Flemish dialects seemed supremely well suited, as they had preserved the medieval heritage virtually intact. In Gezelle's opinion only this „ancient" form of Dutch was able to offer the necessary protection against foreign intruders threatening the Flemish character and people, i.e. against both the „half-heathen speech of Holland" and the liberal and libertine French.

Others, like Jan Frans Willems (1793-1846), the „Father of the Flemish Movement", took a different view. The short-lived union of Belgium and the Netherlands under William I had left them acutely aware of the (distant) common past and the close linguistic affinity between Flanders and the Netherlands. The „integrationists" argued that the standard language of Northern Belgium should be identical with that of the Netherlands. After years of often acrimonious polemic and debate (on, among other things, matters of spelling), the „integrationist" view finally prevailed.

The term „Flemish Movement", generally speaking, cannot be associated with the activities of any one particular group, but denotes rather the struggle of the Flemish people as a whole for recognition of their language and cultural aspirations. Although initially the objectives of the Flemish Movement were mainly of a linguistic and literary nature, by the end of the 19th century it had acquired a social and economic dimension as well.

With the gradual socio-economic and political emancipation of the Flemings, the last hundred years or so have brought far-reaching legislation granting the Dutch language in the Flemish provinces exclusive rights in the

WOORDENBOEK

DER

NEDERLANDSCHE TAAL,

DOOR

Dʳ. M. DE VRIES EN Dʳ. L. A. TE WINKEL,
LEDEN DER KONINKLIJKE ACADEMIE VAN WETENSCHAPPEN.

EERSTE AFLEVERING.

'S GRAVENHAGE, LEIDEN, ARNHEM,
MARTINUS NIJHOFF, A. W. SIJTHOFF, D. A. THIEME.

BATAVIA.   BRUSSEL, GENT.   KAAPSTAD.
G. KOLFF & COMP.   C. MUQUARDT, W. ROGGHÉ.   J. C. JUTA.

1864.

„Woordenboek der Nederlandsche Taal", 1864.

WOORDENLIJST

VAN DE

NEDERLANDSE

TAAL

SAMENGESTELD IN OPDRACHT VAN DE
NEDERLANDSE
EN DE
BELGISCHE REGERING

'S-GRAVENHAGE
STAATSDRUKKERIJ- EN UITGEVERIJBEDRIJF
1954

„Woordenlijst van de Nederlandse Taal", 1954

judicial, administrative and educational sphere and in the army. Starting in the 1870's, a succession of hard-won legislative measures gave Dutch a modest niche in the courts of justice, administration and state education. The „Equality Law" of 1898 recognized Dutch as one of the two official languages of Belgium, on a par with French. In 1930 the State University of Ghent adopted Dutch as its language of instruction, and in 1932 primary and secondary education in Flanders became exclusively Dutch-speaking. The whole process has often provoked bitter resistance in French-speaking circles, as was shown again by the tumultuous reception of the decree of 19 July 1973 (issued by the Cultural Council of the Dutch-language Community, the authoritative body for all cultural matters in Flanders) which stipulated that Dutch was to be the sole medium in all exchanges between employers and employees in the Dutch-speaking region. The crowning achievement in the long struggle for the recognition of Dutch as the only standard language of the Flemish part of Belgium, was the decree of 10 December 1973, which confirmed that the official designation of the language spoken in Flanders is „Dutch, or the Dutch language".

The growing co-operation between North and South

A few decades after the Belgian Revolution, Dutch and Flemish linguists took steps to renew their former contacts. From 1849 onwards they held joint conferences. They also planned the publication of a monumental *Woordenboek der Nederlandsche Taal,* (Dictionary of the Dutch Language), the first instalment of which appeared in 1864. The Dictionary required a uni-

de Nederlandse
TAALUNIE

Zijne Majesteit de Koning der Belgen en
Hare Majesteit de Koningin der Nederlanden;

Zich bewust van het belang van de Nederlandse taal voor de
samenleving in Hun landen;

Zich ervan bewust dat de overheden van Hun landen samen
medeverantwoordelijk zijn voor de Nederlandse taal als
instrument van maatschappelijk verkeer en als
uitdrukkingsmiddel van wetenschap en letteren, alsmede voor
de vaardigheid in het gebruik ervan;

Ervan overtuigd dat grotere bekendheid met de Nederlandse
taal en letteren in het buitenland zal leiden tot meer waardering
voor de Nederlandse cultuur;

Ervan overtuigd dat de gemeenschappelijke zorg voor de
Nederlandse taal de banden tussen de Nederlandstaligen in
Hun landen zal versterken;

Erkennend dat het Verdrag betreffende de culturele en
intellectuele betrekkingen tussen het Koninkrijk België en het
Koninkrijk der Nederlanden, dat op 16 mei 1946 tussen Hun
landen is gesloten, de onderlinge betrekkingen in grote mate
heeft bevorderd en mede heeft geleid tot een hechtere
samenwerking tussen de Nederlandstaligen in Hun landen;

Verlangend, in het licht van het voorgaande, aan Hun
samenwerking op het gebied van de Nederlandse taal een
meer institutioneel karakter te geven;

Hebben besloten tot de instelling van een unie op het gebied
van de Nederlandse taal en hebben hiertoe als Hun
gevolmachtigden aangewezen:

The Dutch Language Union, a treaty between the Kingdom of Belgium and the Kingdom of the Netherlands, signed in Brussels on 9th September, 1980.

form spelling, and the system designed by the Dutchmen M. de Vries and L.A. te Winkel was officially adopted in Belgium in 1864 and in the Netherlands in 1883. After joint consultation between the Dutch and Belgian governments a simplified spelling system was introduced in both countries in 1946, and the official spellinglist (*Woordenlijst van de Nederlandse taal*) appeared in 1954.

Since 1946 the cultural integration of the Netherlands and Flanders has been actively promoted by various official and private initiatives. Among the latter we can mention the „Algemeen Nederlands Verbond" (Pan-Dutch League), the „Komitee voor Frans-Vlaanderen" (Committee for French-Flanders), which strives to preserve the Flemish character of French-Flanders, the Flemish-Netherlands foundation „Stichting Ons Erfdeel" (Our Heritage), which publishes two cultural magazines, one in Dutch, also called *Ons Erfdeel,* the other in French and called *Septentrion, revue de culture néerlandaise,* the Foundation „Stichting Lodewijk de Raet", which is concerned primarily with socio-economic questions, etc.

On 9 September 1980 the Netherlands and Belgium signed the articles of the „Nederlandse Taalunie" (Dutch Language Union), which is founded on the unity of the language spoken and written in the Netherlands and the Dutch-speaking part of Belgium. The Dutch language is crucial to the life of both countries and to co-operation between them, and both governments believe they have a joint responsibility for its development.

An important result of co-operation within the Dutch Language Union has been the publication of the *Algemene Nederlandse Spraakkunst* (1984), an extensive reference grammar written jointly by Flemish and Dutch linguists.

Van Dale.
Groot Woordenboek der
Nederlandse taal, 1984.

Algemene Nederlandse
Spraakkunst, 1984.

However, the official recognition that Dutch is the common language of the Netherlands and Flanders does not mean that all linguistic differences within the Dutch-language area have been completely erased. These differences are a natural consequence of the fact that various local dialects coexist within the language. The Amsterdam accent differs from Groningen speech, the dialect of Bruges is not that of Hasselt. In any case, these are differences that exist in every language; German does not sound quite the same in Hamburg and in Munich, the English heard in London is distinct from that spoken in York, the Parisian accent is different from that of Bordeaux.

And yet, the foreign visitor with an ear for language will soon notice that even Standard Dutch as it is spoken in the Netherlands does not sound quite the same as the Standard Dutch spoken in Flanders. Three centuries of political and cultural separation have, inevitably, left their mark. In the North, Standard Dutch has enjoyed a steady development from the 17th century onwards, in close relation with the local dialects. But in Flanders, until well into the 20th century, the Dutch dialects led a fragmented and isolated existence, while the standard language was a foreign tongue, French. As a result the dialects of Northern Belgium borrowed liberally from that foreign tongue, and even today the Standard Dutch spoken and written in Flanders has not yet entirely shaken off the effects of interference from French.

Nevertheless it would be quite wrong to speak of two languages. At most there are two variants of the same language, and the differences between them are becoming less significant all the time. The closer and more numerous personal contacts between the Netherlands and Flanders, the role of the mass media, Dutch-language education in Flanders, the continuing activities of cultural associations in both Flanders and the Netherlands, the growing use of Standard Dutch in young families in Flanders, all these factors must in the long run bring about the unity of the Dutch language and, in the process, also increase the contribution of Flanders to the common tongue.

The use of Dutch in the Netherlands and Flanders stimulates cultural integration within the Golden Delta, and as the European Community grows and develops, this integration, too, is taking firmer shape.

Surrounded by three large language areas - English, French and German - a community of some 20 million Europeans shares a single common language: Dutch.

Appendices

Appendix 1

Some linguistic characteristics

For English-speaking readers, who may have some knowledge of German, the following observations will serve to illustrate certain special features of Dutch.

Pronunciation

The Dutch language makes use of a number of sounds which are not found in other related languages, including English and German. One of these sounds is the [ɣ], as in the word „geven" (to give); it is the voiced counterpart to the voiceless velar fricative [x] in English „loch", German „lachen", Spanish „jerez" (in Northern speech [ɣ] tends to be pronounced as [x]). Typical of Dutch is also the consonant cluster [sx], as in „school" (school). And then there are the diphthongs [e.w], as in „eeuw" (century); [i.w], in „nieuw" (new); [o.i], in „mooi" (beautiful); [y.w], in „duw" (push); [u.i], in „boei" (buoy); and [œ.y], in „zuil" (pillar).

In contrast with English, all final consonants in Dutch words become voiceless. Thus „ik heb" and „ik had" (I have, I had) are pronounced [ɪkhɛp] and [ɪkhɑt], and there is no difference in pronunciation between „(hij) velt" (he fells) and „(het) veld" (the field), which is in both cases [vɛlt], between „hard" (hard) and „hart" (heart), which are both pronounced [hɑrt], or between „lach" (smile, laughter) and „(ik) lag" (I lay), both pronounced [lɑx].

An important factor in the pronunciation of Dutch is the part played by assimilation, i.e. the mutual modification of adjacent consonants. A few examples will illustrate the point. The list below gives in each case two words, indicating first (on the left) the pronunciation of the final consonant of the first word and of the initial consonant of the second word, and then (on the right) the pronunciation of the same consonants when they occur in adjacent positions (either within one compound word, or in different but contiguous words):

af [f] and [b] breken	afbreken [vb] (to break off)
kap [p] and [b] blok	kapblok [b] (chopping-block)
op [p] and [d] duiken	opduiken [bd] (to emerge, to surface)
het [t] and [d] dal	het dal [d] (the valley)
ik [k] and [z] zal	ik zal [ks] (I shall)
af [f] and [ɣ] geven	afgeven [fx] (to deliver)
is [s] and [v] vol	is vol [sf] (is full)
weg [x] and [v] vegen	wegvegen [xf] (to sweep away)

Conclusion:

1. Consonants followed by [b] or [d] become voiced as a result of assimilation; this phenomenon is called anticipatory assimilation.

2. Consonants followed by [z], [ɣ], or [v] do not become voiced; on the contrary, if the first consonant is voiceless, then [z], [ɣ] and [v] also become voiceless. This phenomenon is called progressive assimiliation.

The reasons for this rule are simple: [b] and [d] at the beginning of a word remain unchanged, i.e. voiced. They have phonemic value (i.e. they create distinctions in meaning) in a large number of words. „Breken" (to break) must not be confused with „preken" (to preach), nor „dam" (barrage) with „tam" (tame), „bak" (tray) with „pak" (parcel), „dak" (roof) with „tak" (branch), etc. With [ɣ], [z], and [v] at the beginning of a word the situation is different, as in this case there are only a very few word-pairs where the distinction between voiced and voiceless creates differences in meaning. There are no words at all in the language which distinguish themselves exclusively as a result of having either initial [x] (spelled „ch") or [ɣ] („g"); examples of the other pairs (i.e. distinctions in meaning resulting from words having either initial [v] or [f], or initial [s] or [z]) are extremely rare.

Spelling

Dutch spelling aims at a phonological system, in which each phoneme would ideally be represented by its own symbol. In a fully consistent phonological spelling, however, the number of symbols would multiply rapidly, thus needlessly complicating the appearance of the written language. The spelling of Dutch, then, obeys a limited number of principles and rules which complement and restrict one another. The main principles are these:

- *Uniformity:* a root word is spelled in accordance with the spelling of its derivatives. Although the word „paard" (horse) is pronounced [pa.rt], we spell it with a „-d" because the plural is „paarden" (pronounced [pa.rdən]). Similarly, we write „weg" (pronounced [wɛx]), because the plural is „wegen" (pronounced [we.ɣ ən]).

- *Etymology:* in many cases the spelling reflects etymological differences between particular words even though at present their pronunciation may be identical. We write, for example, „zei" (said) and „zij" (she, they), both pronounced [zɛ.j], and „rauw" (raw) and „rouw" (mourning), both pronounced [rɔ.w], because in each case we are dealing with etymologically different words.

- *Economy:* a long vowel is represented by a double symbol in a closed syllable, but by a single symbol in an open syllable. Hence: „been" (leg), but „benen" (legs), although the pronunciation of the vowel(s) is in both cases [e.]; „laan" and „lanen" (lane, lanes), with both vowels pronounced [a.]; „boom" and „bomen" (tree, trees), both pronounced [o.]; „muur" and „muren" (wall, walls), both pronounced [y.].

- *Foreign words:* words of foreign origin which have become completely integrated into the vocabulary of Dutch (the so-called loan-words) will eventually be adapted to the rules of Dutch spelling in so far as their pronunciation permits such an operation. We have the choice between writing „consequent" (consistent) or „konsekwent", but words like „bureau" and „cake" still retain - for the time being - their original French and English spelling. Some solutions, though, remain half-hearted, as in „elektricien" (from the French „électricien", electrician), where the „k" is consistent with pronunciation, but the „c" is pronounced [s]!

Word order

In some cases Dutch offers two possibilities for placing the parts of compound verbal constructions in subordinate clauses. In this respect Dutch occupies an intermediate position between English and German. One brief example will suffice:

English: the book (which) he has received ...
Dutch: het boek dat hij heeft ontvangen ...
or: het boek dat hij ontvangen heeft ...
German: das Buch, das er empfangen hat ...

Inflection and declension

The old inflectional system of Germanic has been radically simplified in Dutch. In this respect Dutch has gone further than German, though not quite as far as English.

The definite article has two forms: „de" (masculine and feminine) and „het" (neuter), whereas English has only one („the") and German still has six („der, die, das, des, dem,

46

den"). The most common plural endings of substantives in Dutch are „-(e)n" and „-s". Here again Dutch has two forms where English has only one („-s") and German has several more („-e", „-̈e", „-er", „-̈er", „-(e)n", „-", „-̈"). The strong verb in Dutch has retained eight forms (of which only six are commonly used), as e.g. in the verb „vallen" (to fall): „vallen, (valle), val, valt, viel, (vielt), vielen, gevallen". The English strong verb has fewer: „(to) fall, falls, fell, fallen", but German has more: „fallen, falle, fällst, fällt, fallt, fiel, fielst, fielt, fielen, fiele, fielest, fielet, gefallen".

Similarly, the two forms of the Dutch adjective („goed, goede") occupy an intermediate position between the unchanging English form („good") and the more numerous German ones („gut, guter, gute, gutes, gutem, guten").

Derivations and compound words

All Germanic languages share the ability to form derivatives and compound words on the basis of a single kernel word. Dutch makes a decidedly liberal use of this linguistic feature. A well-known example is the list of more than thirty derivatives and compounds built around the kernel „god"; among the most common of these are: goddeloos (godless), goddelijk (divine), godvruchtig (devout), godsdienst (religion), godgeleerdheid (theology), de godganse dag (all day long), 't is godgeklaagd (it's a crying shame), godslamp (sanctuary lamp), godsonmogelijk (absolutely impossible), etc. Or, to take a less pious example, some of the combinations with „hei" and „heien" (pile-driver; to pile the ground): heiblok (pilinghammer), heimachine (pile-driver), heipaal (pile), heiploeg (piling-crew), heistelling (pile-frame), heitouw (lifting-rope), heiwerk (pile-driving), handhei (hand pile-driver), trekhei (common-ram), klinkhei (pile-driver with pincers), stoomhei (steam pile-driver), stoomheimachine (steam pile-driver) etc.

Vocabulary

In some fields of science Dutch has an indigenous terminology, in most cases dating from the late 16th and early 17th century, when the trend towards purism played such an important part in the formation of Standard Dutch. Simon Stevin (1548-1620), for example, enriched the language with a number of geometrical and mathematical terms made up of native Dutch words, where English relies on Latin and/or Greek elements. Thus he introduced veelhoek (literally: „multi-angle") for polygon, driehoek for triangle, vijfhoek for pentagon, etc.; other terms too, like middellijn („middle-line") for diameter, aftrekken („take away") for subtract, breuk („fracture") for fraction, noemer („namer") for denominator (of a fraction), etc., appeal immediately to the native speaker's imagination. The internationally renowned legal expert Hugo de Groot (1583-1645) invented terms like roerend en onroerend goed (personal property and real estate), erfpacht (hereditary tenure), winstderving (loss of profit), etc.

It will surprise no-one to hear that the vocabulary of Dutch shows the influence of various other languages. This kind of lexical give-and-take, of influencing others and being influenced in turn, is a common feature of all West European languages, although some may have borrowed more liberally than others (may be more „open" than others). Dutch ranks among the languages which have borrowed freely, for a number of reasons: its proximity to three powerful neighbours: English, French and German; the close trading relations with the rest of the world; the colonial past, which took the Dutch to North America (New Amsterdam, now New York), to Surinam and the Antilles (where Dutch is still the language of education and the administration), to South Africa, to Indonesia, etc.; and the - mostly uninvited - presence of foreign armies (Spanish, Austrian, French, ...) at various stages in the history of the Low Countries. All these factors have left their mark on the language, and first and foremost on its vocabulary.

Even before Dutch emerged as a separate language, *Latin* and, through Latin, *Greek* had already enriched the Germanic tongues with numerous words pertaining to all spheres of daily life. After the fall of the Roman Empire the Christian Church took over the role of the Roman soldiers and colonizers. During the Renaissance era another wave of Latin and Greek words invaded the languages of Western Europe. And at present many of our newer technological terms are made up of words of Latin and/or Greek stock.

From the Middle Ages onwards, *French* also became an important influence. The court of the Counts of Flanders was bilingual. The late-medieval Chambers of Rhetoric made abundant use of lexical borrowings and adaptations from French in their never-ending search for rhyme-words. During the 17th and 18th centuries the impact of French culture made itself felt throughout Europe, and again Dutch, like other European languages, saw no objection to borrowing.

In the 13th century *Italian* bankers and businessmen settled in Dutch and Flemish towns, and during the Renaissance Flemish and Dutch artists in their turn went to Italy as apprentices. This explains the (fairly small) number of Italian-derived commercial and artistic words in Dutch. The close political and cultural relations between the Low Countries and Spain in the 16th and 17th centuries have also left some *Spanish* traces in Dutch.

The *German* contribution to the Dutch vocabulary dates mainly from the period of the Reformation, although some of the medieval mystics (e.g., Hadewijch) had already adopted a number of words from their German predecessors. The first Protestant Bible to appear in Dutch (in 1523) was a translation of Martin Luther's New Testament. A number of German military terms also passed into Dutch in the 16th century.

English was a relative latecomer, but when its influence finally made itself felt, it did so with a vengeance. In spite of a few words dating from the early days of the newspaper business and from the era of the Industrial Revolution, the number of borrowings remained fairly small until the Second World War. Since then, however, the economic and technological supremacy of the United States in the Western World has led to an unstoppable flood of Anglo-American words. At present the language of the mass media, of the social and exact sciences, of the world of business, sports, music and fashion, is teeming with English coinages and loan-words. Although the English words mostly pass into Dutch intact (as is the case with, say, multinational, planning, manager, computer, interview, insider, coach, etc.), some are partly integrated and made to comply with the rules of word-formation in Dutch („to run a firm" becomes „een bedrijf runnen", „de gehandicapten" means „handicapped people", etc.), or adopt new meanings („een dancing" means „a dance-hall", etc.); still others may be translated, wholly (Dutch has „weekend", but also „weekeind" and „weekeinde"; „showroom", but also „toonkamer" and „toonzaal"), or in part (which produces odd hybrids like „bandrecorder" alongside „tape-recorder" and „bandopnemer", etc.).

The impact of Dutch on other languages

As was pointed out above, lexical items migrate from one language to another. Languages give and take words, they lend and borrow. The economic prosperity of Flanders in the Middle Ages and of Holland in the 17th century has left its traces in various other languages. As a result of international trade hundreds of Dutch words, many of them nautical terms, have passed into foreign languages.

English has a fair number of words of Dutch origin: to beleaguer („belegeren"), boor („boer"), boss („baas"), brandy („brandewijn", burnt, i.e. distilled wine), bulwark („bolwerk"), bundle („bundel"), buoy („boei"), (ca)boodle („boedel", possessions), crimp („krimpen", to shrink), dock

(„dok"), drill („drillen", to bore, drill a hole), easel („ezel", ass), freight („vracht"), to keelhaul („kielhalen"), landscape („landschap"), manikin (middle Dutch „mannikin", little man), to prate („praten", to talk), scrabble (Middle Dutch „scrabben", to scrape), sketch („schets"), snack (originally a snap or a bite, from Middle Dutch „snacken", a variant of „snappen", to snap, catch), splinter („splinter"), spook („spook", ghost), whiting („wijting"), yacht („jacht").

Some words passed from Dutch into English via French: droll, drollery come via French „drôle" from Middle Dutch „drolle", little man; the words freebooter and filibuster are both derived from Dutch „vrijbuiter", but the first one is a direct borrowing, whereas the second came via French („flibustier") and/or Spanish („filibustero"). Others passed into English via Afrikaans: aardvark, aardwolf, apartheid, Boer, Bushman, dingus, kraal, springbok, trek, veld, wildebeest, etc. (For Afrikaans, see Appendix 3).

Among the Dutch loan-words in *French* we find s'affaler („afhalen", to lower, pull down), bague (dial. „bagge", ring), bouquin („boeckin", little book), clamp („klamp", clamp), colza („koolzaad", rapeseed), épisser („splitsen", to splice a rope), estompe („stomp", dull), foc („fok", foresail), fret („vrecht", „vracht", freight), haler („halen", to haul), hier („heien", to pile the ground), hisser („hijsen", to lift), houblon („hoppe", hops), hourque („hoeker", a type of cargo ship), kermesse („kermis", fair), matelot („matroos", sailor), plaquer („plakken", to paste, glue), potasse („potas", potash), prame („praam", pram, lighter), etc.

Other Dutch words passed via French into *Italian* and *Spanish:* amarrer, ammarare, amarrar („maren, meren", to moor), bâbord, babordo, babor („bakboord", portside), beaupré, bompresso, beauprés („boegspriet", bowsprit), étape, tappa, etapa („stapel", stock, storehouse), mannequin, manichino, maniquí („mannekijn", model).

The word mannequin (model) is a special case: having first been borrowed from Middle Dutch mannikin (little man), it subsequently passed back into Dutch with its French form and meaning!

German words directly borrowed from Dutch are, for example: Augenmerk (from Dutch „oogmerk", aim, intention), Auster („oester", oyster), Bücherei („boekerij", library), Fracht („vracht", freight), Klippe („klip", cliff), Matrose („matroos", sailor), Schauburg (in Hannover and Hamburg) („schouwburg", theatre), Stapel(platz) („stapel(plaats)", store-house), etc.

Through the ages *Russian* sailors, too, appear to have picked up a smattering of Dutch. Czar Peter the Great's visit to Zaandam in 1697, and the trading links between Holland and the Baltic in the 17th century (the „home trade", as it was known) are responsible for the presence of several nautical terms of Dutch origin in Russian. Among these are bom (from Dutch „boom", barrier, boom), blok („blok", pulley-block), botsman („bootsman", boatswain), buy („boei", buoy), drek („dreg", drag, grapnel), forshteven („voorsteven", stem [of a ship]), gals („hals", neck), gavan („haven", port), matros („matroos", sailor), shturman („stuurman", helmsman, navigator), verf („werf", shipyard), verpovat („werpanker", kedge), yakhta („jacht", yacht).

Dutch even penetrated as far as *Japan*. From 1639 until 1853 the Dutch were the only Europeans with whom the Japanese had direct contacts. Western science was known as „Dutch science", and scientific books were translated into Japanese via Dutch. Among the Dutch loan-words in Japanese are biiru („bier", beer), buriki („blik", tin, tin plate), gomu („gom", gum), inki (from Dutch „inkt", ink), kohii („koffie", coffee), kiniine („kinine", quinine), koruku („kurk", cork), mesu („mes", knife), supoitu (Dutch „spuit", syringe, sprayer), tarappu („trap", staircase), etc.

Equally worth mentioning is the impact of Dutch on both *Sinhalese,* the principal language of Sri Lanka (formerly Ceylon), which from 1656 to 1802 was a Dutch colony, and on *Indonesian,* the Malay-based national language created in 1949, when the Dutch left Indonesia after almost 350 years of colonial rule. As an official language Dutch was then replaced by Indonesian, but apart from English it has remained the most frequently used commercial language.

In conclusion, it should be mentioned that Dutch is an official language of the *Dutch Antilles,* which are still part of the Kingdom of the Netherlands, and of *Surinam,* which became an independent country in 1975. Both in the Dutch Antilles and Surinam there is a literature in Dutch.

••••••••	Dutch-French language border in Belgium
– – –	Provincial boundaries.
——	National frontiers.
B	Brussels: bilingual area (Dutch-French)

[dotted]	West-Flemish and Zealand dialects
[hatched]	Brabant and East-Flemish dialects
[vertical lines]	Holland dialects.
[horizontal lines]	Limburg dialects.
[stippled]	Saxon dialects
[blank]	Frisian dialects.
[crosshatched]	Mixed dialect areas.

This division of Dutch dialects into major groups is based on differences and correspondences in phonology, morphology, syntax and vocabulary. Modern dialectologists, notably Prof. A. Weijnen, give the groups new, neutral designations, but the traditional ones have been retained here.

Appendix 2

The Dutch dialects

Dutch has a great many local dialects, but they can be subsumed under a few main groups with common characteristics. The traditional names for these groups were derived from the various Germanic tribes who settled in these regions after the fall of the Roman Empire (namely the Franks, the Saxons and the Frisians). A modern dialectologist like Prof. A. Weijnen prefers to use neutral, purely geographical designations such as „north-eastern", „central southern", etc. In the brief survey below we have adopted Prof. Weijnen's classification (which is based on similarities and differences in phonology, morphology, syntax and vocabulary), while preserving some of the traditional names:

1. The *West-Flemish and Zealand (or south-western) dialects* are spoken in three different countries: in the Dutch province of Zealand-Flanders (except for the eastern part), in most parts of West Flanders (Belgium), and in French-Flanders (where in spite of the fact that the area has been part of France for some 300 years now, an estimated 100,000 people still speak or at least understand the dialect).

2. The *Brabant (or southern central) dialects,* which are spoken in the Belgian provinces of East Flanders, Antwerp, and (Flemish) Brabant, in the Dutch province of North Brabant, and in the southernmost area of Gelderland.

3. The *(northern central) dialects of Holland,* spoken in the Dutch provinces of North and South Holland, and Utrecht.

4. The *Limburg (or south-eastern) dialects,* in both the Belgian and Dutch provinces of Limburg.

5. The *Saxon (or north-eastern) dialects,* in the Dutch provinces of Groningen, Drenthe, Overijssel, and the northern part of Gelderland.

6. The *Frisian dialects,* which strictly speaking are not Dutch dialects at all, since Frisian must be regarded as a separate language. On the whole the Frisian dialects are historically closer to English than to either Dutch or German.

Appendix 3

Afrikaans

In 1652 three ships belonging to the Dutch East India Company cast anchor in a bay at the foot of Table Mountain, near the Cape of Good Hope. The Europeans aboard the ships were under the command of the Dutchman Jan van Riebeeck. Their task was the establishment and manning of a supply station for ships on their way to the Indies and back. Van Riebeeck's companions were for the most part sailors and farmers from the provinces of Holland and Zealand. Their seventeenth-century dialects formed the basis of the present Afrikaans language, which to many Dutch-speakers resembles a kind of simplified Dutch. The reasons for this grammatical simplification have been explained in different ways, some linguists emphasizing the influence of other languages (native African tongues, Malay, English, ...), others stressing the internal dynamic of Afrikaans itself.

Until well into the 19th century the Boers wrote what must be described as incorrect Dutch. They had very little contact with the spoken Dutch of the mother country, and kept in touch with written Dutch only through the seventeenth-century text of the States Bible. In the course of the 19th century the gap between the Boers' everyday speech and the written Dutch coming to them from Europe had become unbridgeable. As a result, a tendency began to emerge favouring recognition of the popular speech of the Boers as a written language, too. In the opinion of the Boers this was also the only way to resist the growing pressure of English. To this end the „Genootschap van Regte Afrikaners" (Association of True Afrikaners) was founded in 1875, and with it the „First Afrikaner Movement" was born.

After the Boer wars, the Union of South Africa, which joined together the former Boer Republics and the English possessions in that part of the continent, still declared Dutch and English to be the two official languages of the new state. In 1925 Afrikaans replaced Dutch.

Today, Afrikaans is the native language of some 60 % of the whites in South Africa, and of about 90 % of its Coloured population (meaning, not the black population, but those of mixed descent, i.e. Hottentot and white, and Asian and white). Whites and Coloureds together make up some 5 million Afrikaans-speakers in a total population of about 25 million.

Appendix 4

Bibliography

1. Dictionaries

Bilingual dictionaries

Engels Woordenboek. Compiled by K. ten Bruggencate & A. Broers. 2 vols. Groningen, Wolters-Noordhoff, 1984 (19th ed.).

Kramers' Engels Woordenboek. Compiled by J.A. Jockin-la Bastide & G. van Kooten. 2 vols. The Hague, van Goor (1978) (vol. 1), Amsterdam/Brussels, Elsevier, 1979 (vol. 2) (36th ed.).

Nieuw groot Nederlands-Engels Woordenboek voor studie en praktijk. Compiled by H. Jansonius. 3 vols. Leiden, Nederlandse Uitgeversmaatschappij, 1972-73.

Standaard groot Engels-Nederlands Woordenboek. Compiled by B.J. Wevers & P.J. Verhoeff. Antwerp, Standaard, 1974.

Standaard Nederlands-Engels woordenboek. Compiled by P.J. Verhoeff & B.J. Wevers. Antwerp, Standaard, 1982.

Van Dale. Groot woordenboek Engels-Nederlands. Compiled by W. Martin and G.A.J. Tops. Utrecht/Antwerp, Van Dale Lexicografie, 1984.

Van Dale. Groot woordenboek Nederlands-Engels. Compiled by W. Martin and G.A.J. Tops. Utrecht/Antwerp, Van Dale Lexicografie, 1986.

Pocket dictionaries, learner's dictionaries and word-lists

Basiswoordenboek Nederlands. Compiled by P. de Kleijn & E. Nieuwborg. Leuven, Wolters, 1983.

A Dutch Vocabulary. Compiled by B.C. Donaldson. Melbourne, AE Press, 1983.

Leerwoordenboek voor buitenlanders. Compiled by J. Hart & H. Polter, Groningen, Wolters-Noordhoff, 1983.

Prisma handwoordenboek Engels-Nederlands, Nederlands-Engels. Compiled by F.J.J. Baars, et al. 2 vols. Antwerp/Utrecht, 1983[16].

A. Ryckaert's Standaard Nederlands-Engels, Engels-Nederlands zakwoordenboek. Antwerp, Standaard, 1973.

2000 woorden. Basiswoordenboek Engels-Nederlands. Compiled by P.H. Collin, R. Helsloot & E. Reichling. London, Harrap, 1983.

Woordenlijst elementaire kennis. Compiled by F. Beersmans & I. Beheydt. Brussels, Commissariaat-Generaal voor de Internationale Samenwerking/The Hague, Ministerie van Onderwijs en Wetenschappen, 1983.

Woordenlijst van de Nederlandse taal. Compiled by C.B. van Haeringen, et al. The Hague, Staatsuitgeverij, 1954.

Special dictionaries

Engels handelswoordenboek. Compiled by A. Bons. Deventer, Kluwer, 1957².

Kluwer's Universeel Technisch Woordenboek. Compiled by G. Schuurmans Stekhoven. 2 vols. (E-D, D-E). Deventer/ Antwerp, Kluwer, 1977.

Standaard Nederlands-Engels technisch woordenboek. Compiled by H.J.W. Peek. Antwerp, Standaard, 1974.

Technisch Engels woordenboek, Nederlands-Engels en Engels-Nederlands. Compiled by H. Jansonius. Leiden, Nederlandse Uitgeversmaatschappij, 1965.

Nederlands Etymologisch Woordenboek. Compiled by J. de Vries and F. de Tollenaere. E.J. Brill, Leiden, 1963-1971.

Etymologisch Woordenboek. Compiled by J. de Vries. Revised by F. de Tollenaere. Spectrum. Utrecht/Antwerpen, 1983¹³.

A Dictionary of the Low-Dutch Element in the English Vocabulary. Compiled by J.F. Bense. The Hague, M. Nijhoff, 1939.

Dutch-language dictionaries

Woordenboek der Nederlandse Taal. Begun by M. de Vries & L.A. te Winkel. 24 vols. (A-V); still incomplete. The Hague, M. Nijhoff, 1864-.

Van Dale. Groot woordenboek der Nederlandse Taal. Revised by G. Geerts, H. Heestermans and C. Kruyskamp. 3 vols. Utrecht/ Antwerp, Van Dale Lexicografie, 1984¹¹.

Van Dale Groot Woordenboek van hedendaags Nederlands. Compiled by P.G.J. van Sterkenburg and W.J.J. Pijnenburg. Utrecht/ Antwerp, Van Dale Lexicografie, 1984.

Het juiste woord. Betekeniswoordenboek der Nederlandse taal. Compiled by L. Brouwers. Antwerp/Utrecht, Standaard, 1973⁵.

Signalement van nieuwe woorden. Compiled by R. Reinsma. Amsterdam/Brussels, Elsevier, 1975.

ABN-uitspraakgids. Compiled by P.C. Paardekooper. Hasselt, Heideland-Orbis, 1978.

Groot uitspraakwoordenboek van de Nederlandse taal. Compiled by R.H.B. de Coninck. Antwerp, De Nederlandsche Boekhandel, 1970.

Koenen. Verklarend handwoordenboek der Nederlandse taal. Revised by J.B. Drewes. Groningen, Wolters-Noordhoff, 1975 [27].

2. Audio-visual courses and aids

Actief Nederlands. (textbook, illustrations, teacher's handbook). Compiled by F. van Passel. 3 vols. Antwerp, De Sikkel, 1971[2].

Audiovisuele Methode Nederlands. (textbooks, illustrations, tapes, filmstrips). Compiled by M.J. de Vriendt-de Man, S. de Vriendt, J. Eggermont, M. Wambach, C. Wuilmart, H. Schutte. Brussels, Didier, 1967-70.

Dutch in Three Months. (textbook, cassettes). Compiled by J.K. Fenoulhet. London, Hugo's Language Books, 1985[2].

Levend Nederlands. Een audio-visuele cursus Nederlands voor buitenlanders. (textbook, tapes, filmstrips). Compiled by the Department of Linguistics, Cambridge University, and the Afdeling Toegepaste Taalwetenschap, Free University of Amsterdam. Cambridge/London/New York/Melbourne, Cambridge University Press, second revised edition, 1984.

Linguaphone Dutch. (textbooks, cassettes). London, Linguaphone Institute, second revised edition, 1984.

Nederlands in beeld en klank. (textbook, illustrations, teacher's handbook, filmstrips, tapes). Compiled by R. Maréchal & G. van Straelen-van Rintel. Brussels, Didier, 1971.

Speak Dutch. (textbooks, records or cassettes). Compiled by W. Lagerwey. Amsterdam, Meulenhoff, 1973[4].

Spoken Dutch. (textbooks, records or cassettes). Compiled by L. Bloomfield. New York, Holt, Rinehart & Winston, 1973[2].

An English Self-Study Supplement to Levend Nederlands. Compiled by J.H. Hulstijn & M. Hannay. Amsterdam, V.U. Boekhandel/Uitgeverij, 1981.

3. Textbook courses, grammars and readers

BIRD, R.B., & SHETTER, W.Z. *Reading Dutch. Fifteen Annotated Stories from the Low Countries.* Leiden, M. Nijhoff, 1985.

DE JONGHE, H. and DE GEEST, W. *Nederlands, je taal.* Lier, Van In, 1985.

DONALDSON, B.C. *Dutch Reference Grammar.* The Hague, M. Nijhoff, 1981.

GEERTS, G., HAESERYN, W., DE ROOIJ, J., VAN DEN TOORN, M.C., eds. *Algemene Nederlandse Spraakkunst*. Groningen, Wolters-Noordhoff/Leuven, Wolters, 1984.

KOOLHOVEN, H. *Teach Yourself Dutch*. London, Teach Yourself Books, 1974.

LAMBREGTSE, C. *Fundamentals of Practical Dutch Grammar*. Grand Rapids (Michigan), Eerdmans, 1965.

RENIER, F.G. *Learn Dutch!* London, Routledge & Kegan Paul, 1970.

SCHOENMAKERS, A. *Praatpaal. Dutch for Beginners*. Cheltenham, S. Thornes, 1981.

SHETTER, W.Z. *Introduction to Dutch*. Leiden, M. Nijhoff, 1984[5].

SMIT, J. & MEIJER, R.P. *Dutch Grammar and Reader*. Cheltenham, S. Thornes, 1976[4].

TOORN-DAMMER, N. VAN DEN. *Basisgrammatika voor het Nederlands als vreemde taal*. Amsterdam, Koninklijk Instituut voor de Tropen, n.d.

WILLIAMS, J.K. *A Dutch Reader*. Cheltenham, S. Thornes, 1981.

WILMOTS, J. *Voor wie Nederlands wil leren*. (2 vols.) Diepenbeek, Economische Hogeschool Limburg, 1974[2].

4. Works on the Dutch language

BERG B. VAN DEN. *Foniek van het Nederlands*. The Hague, Van Goor, 1972.

BRACHIN, P. *The Dutch Language. A Survey*. Cheltenham, S. Thornes, 1985.

COLLINS, B. & MEES, I. *The Sounds of English and Dutch*. Leiden, Leiden University Press, 1984[2].

DAAN, J., DEPREZ, K., HOUT, R. VAN, STROOP, J. *Onze veranderende taal*. Utrecht/Antwerp, Spectrum, 1985.

DONALDSON, B.C. *Dutch. A Linguistic History of Holland and Belgium*. Leiden, M. Nijhoff, 1983.

GEERTS, G. *Voorlopers en varianten van het Nederlands. Een gedokumenteerd dia- en synchroon overzicht*. Leuven, Acco, 1975.

HAERINGEN, C.B. VAN. *Netherlandic Language Research. Men and Works in the Study of Dutch*. Leiden, Brill, 1960[2].

HAERINGEN, C.B. VAN. *Nederlands tussen Duits en Engels*. The Hague, Servire, 1966[2].

LOCKWOOD, W.B. *An Informal History of the German Language*. Cambridge, Heffer, 1965. (With chapters on Dutch, Frisian and Afrikaans).

SCHÖNFELD, M. *Historische grammatica van het Nederlands*. Revised by A. van Loey. Zutphen, W.J. Thieme, 1970[8].

SUFFELEERS, T. *Taalverzorging in Vlaanderen. Een opiniegeschiedenis.* Bruges/Nijmegen, Orion/Gottmer, 1979.

TOORN, M.C. VAN DEN. *Nederlandse grammatica.* Groningen, Wolters-Noordhoff, 1977[5].

TOORN, M.C. VAN DEN. *Nederlandse taalkunde.* Utrecht/Antwerp, Spectrum, 1973.

WEIJNEN, A.A. *Nederlandse dialectkunde.* Assen, Van Gorcum, 1966[2].

ZANDVOORT, R.W. *English in the Netherlands. A Linguistic Study in Infiltration.* Groningen, Wolters, 1964.

5. Periodicals

Canadian Journal of Netherlandic Studies. Department of French, University of Windsor, Windsor, Ontario, Canada N9B 3P4.

Dutch Crossing. A Journal of Low Countries Studies. 1977- . Published 3 times a year by the Department of Dutch, University College London, Gower Street, London WCIE 6BT.

Dutch Studies. An Annual Review of the Language, Literature and Life of the Low Countries. 1974-1982. Edited by P. Brachin, P.K. King, J. de Rooij. The Hague, M. Nijhoff.

Delta. A Review of Arts, Life and Thought in the Netherlands. Quarterly, 1958-1973. Amsterdam, Delta International Publishing Foundation.

De Franse Nederlanden / Les Pays-Bas Français. Jaarboek-Annales. Stichting Ons Erfdeel v.z.w., Murissonstraat 260, B-8530 Rekkem.

Neerlandica Extra Muros. 1963-. Halfjaarlijks Tijdschrift van de Internationale Vereniging voor Neerlandistiek, Postbus 84069, 2508 AB The Hague.

Newsletter. American Association for Netherlandic Studies (AANS). Dept. of Germanic Languages, Indiana University, Bloomington, IN 47405.

Ons Erfdeel. Algemeen-Nederlands tweemaandelijks cultureel tijdschrift. Published 5 times a year by the Stichting Ons Erfdeel, Murissonstraat 260, B-8530 Rekkem (Belgium).

Septentrion. Revue de culture néerlandaise. Published 3 times a year by the Stichting Ons Erfdeel (as above).

Details about Dutch literature in translation may be obtained from the *Foundation for Translations* (in full: Foundation for the Promotion of the Translation of Dutch Literary Works), Singel 450, 1017 AV Amsterdam, The Netherlands.

6. General works

BOXER, R. *The Dutch Seaborne Empire 1600-1800.* Harmondsworth, Penguin Books, 1972.

CLOUGH, S.B. *A History of the Flemish Movement in Belgium.* New York, Octagon Books, 1968 (re-issue of 1930 ed.).

DE ROOIJ, J. et al. *Het certificaat Nederlands als vreemde taal.* Brussel, Commissariaat-Generaal voor de Internationale Culturele Samenwerking/The Hague, Ministerie van Onderwijs en Wetenschappen, 1983.

FITZMAURICE, J. *The Politics of Belgium.* London, C. Hurst, 1983.

GOSLINGA, C.C. *A Short History of the Netherlands Antilles and Surinam.* The Hague/Boston/London, M. Nijhoff, 1979.

HUGGETT, B. *Modern Belgium.* London, Pall Mall Press, 1969.

HUGGETT, B. *The Modern Netherlands.* London/New York, Praeger, 1971.

HUIZINGA, J. *Dutch Civilization in the Seventeenth Century, and other Essays.* London, Collins, 1968.

KOSSMANN. E.H. *The Low Countries 1780-1940.* Oxford, The Clarendon Press, 1978.

LIJPHART, A. *The Politics of Accommodation.* Berkeley/Los Angeles/London, University of California Press, 1975[2].

LOVELOCK, Y. *The Line Forward. A Survey of Modern Dutch Poetry in Translation.* Amsterdam, Bridges Books, 1984.

MEIJER, R.P. *Literature of the Low Countries.* Cheltenham, S. Thornes, 1978[2].

NEWTON, G. *The Netherlands. An Historical and Cultural Survey (1795-1977).* London, Benn, 1978.

PARKER, G. *The Dutch Revolt.* Harmondsworth, Penguin Books, 1979.

RUYS, M. *The Flemings. A People on the Move, a Nation in Being.* Tielt/Utrecht, Lannoo, 1973.

SCHÖFFER, I. *A Short History of the Netherlands.* Amsterdam, A. de Lange, 1973[2].

SHETTER, W.Z. *The Pillars of Society. Six Centuries of Civilization in the Netherlands.* The Hague, M. Nijhoff, 1971.

WEEVERS, T. *Poetry of the Netherlands in its European Context, 1170-1930.* London, Athlone, 1960.

WILMOTS, J., & DE ROOIJ, J. (Eds) *Voor wie Nederland en Vlaanderen wil leren kennen.* Diepenbeek, Wetenschappelijk Onderwijs Limburg, 1978.